Children's All-Time Favorite Bible Stories

Shipwrecked!

Peter Pan Talking Books

Paul Sails and Is Shipwrecked and 17 More All-time Favorite Bible Stories from the New Testament

V. Gilbert Beers and Ronald A. Beers

A Peter Pan Talking Book

Below every story there is a QR code linked to the audio recording of that story. Use your phone or camera to scan the QR code to hear the word-for-word audio.

Shipwrecked and 17 More All-time Favorite Bible Stories from the New Testament

Copyright ©2020 Inspired Studios, Inc. All rights reserved.

Published by Inspired Studios, Inc, Boynton Beach, Florida 33473

No part of the publication or recording may be reproduced, distributed, or transmitted in any form or by any means, including photocopying, recording, or other electronic or mechanical methods, without the prior written permission of this publisher.

ISBN 978-0-7396-3802-6

CONTENTS

Peter Heals Aeneas 4

Peter Raises Dorcas from the Dead 6

Cornelius Becomes a Christian 8

Believers at Antioch Called Christians 10

Peter Is Put Into Prison and Escapes 12

Paul Begins His Travels for Jesus 14

Paul and Barnabas Are Mistaken for Gods 16

Paul Is Called to Macedonia 18

Lydia Becomes a Christian 20

The Prison at Philippi 22

The Bereans Accept Paul 24

Paul at Mars Hill 26

Diana of the Ephesians 28

Eutychus Falls from a Window 30

Paul Is Arrested 32

Paul Before Governors and Kings 34

Paul Sails and Is Shipwrecked 36

Paul at Rome 38

Peter Heals Aeneas

Peter traveled through the country, visiting Jesus' followers in different places. One day he stopped in Lydda. Peter met Aeneas there, a man who had been paralyzed for eight years. Aeneas was so crippled that he had to stay in bed all the time.

"Jesus Christ has healed you, Aeneas!" Peter said to him. "Get up and make your bed." Aeneas believed what Peter said. He got up immediately.

All the neighbors in Lydda and even those in the surrounding countryside of Sharon were amazed. When they saw what happened to Aeneas, many of them also believed in Jesus.

Peter Raises Dorcas from the Dead

Tabitha was a wonderful Christian woman who was always helping the poor. Some people called her Dorcas, which meant *gazelle*. Perhaps that was because she was always running around doing special things for people. Dorcas lived in Joppa, just a few miles northwest of Lydda, where Peter had healed Aeneas.

After Dorcas died, her friends washed her body and laid it in an upstairs room. Then they sent two men to Peter. "Come quickly," they urged.

When Peter came to the house, Dorcas's friends took him upstairs to the place where they had put her body. Widows gathered around Peter, crying as they showed him all the cloaks and other clothing Dorcas had made for them. Peter asked everyone to leave the room. Then he knelt and prayed.

"Get up!" he said to Dorcas. Suddenly she opened her eyes, looked at Peter, and sat up. Peter took her by the hand and lifted her up. Then he called the widows and other believers in and presented her to them alive.

Before long, the news of this miracle spread all over Joppa. Many believed in Jesus because of this.

Cornelius Becomes a Christian

One day a Roman army centurion named Cornelius had a vision. He was a godly man in charge of a regiment of soldiers. While Cornelius prayed he saw an angel and heard him speak. "Cornelius!" the angel said.

"What do you want, Lord?" Cornelius answered.

"God wants you to send two men for Peter, who is staying with Simon at Joppa."

As these men were drawing near Joppa the next day, Peter went up to Simon's roof to pray. Suddenly he saw a big sheet, with animals, reptiles, and birds in it. "Kill and eat them," God told Peter.

"No!" said Peter. "These are unclean according to our religious laws. I've never eaten those kinds of things."

"But if I have made something clean, you must not call it unclean," God said.

This happened three times. Then the sheet went away. As soon as that happened the men arrived from Cornelius's house. The Holy Spirit spoke to Peter and told him to go with them.

When Peter went into the house, Cornelius bowed to the floor. "Stand up," said Peter. "I am only a man."

According to Jewish law, Peter should not have been in Cornelius's house, for Cornelius was a Gentile. A Gentile was someone who had not been born a Jew and who did not follow their religious laws. But when Cornelius told Peter about his vision from God and accepted Jesus as Savior, Peter knew God had sent him.

Believers at Antioch Called Christians

When Peter returned to Jerusalem, the Jewish believers criticized him for visiting Cornelius and eating with his friends and relatives. They had already heard about this, and they had heard how the Gentiles had accepted Jesus as their Savior.

Then Peter explained the whole story to them. He told them about his vision, and how Cornelius had also had a vision from God. When they heard this, they were glad and stopped their criticism.

About the same time more Gentiles were accepting Jesus as Savior at Antioch. The church at Jerusalem sent Barnabas there to see what was happening. When he saw how God was working, he encouraged the believers there to keep on with their good work.

Then he went to Tarsus, found Saul, and brought him back to Antioch to work. Barnabas and Saul stayed there for a year, working with the church at Antioch. It was there that believers were first called Christians.

While Barnabas and Saul were at Antioch, a prophet named Agabus came with some other prophets from Jerusalem. He predicted a famine would spread over the Roman Empire, and it actually happened during the time when Claudius was emperor.

The Christians at Antioch decided they would take a collection for the Christians in Judea and Jerusalem. So they did this and sent it there with Barnabas and Saul.

Peter Is Put Into Prison and Escapes

King Herod began to arrest the Christians and persecute them. He executed John's brother, James, with a sword. He put Peter in prison and put a guard of four squads of four soldiers each to watch him. After the Passover, he would put Peter on trial.

The Christians began to pray earnestly while Peter was in prison. The night before Peter would go on trial, he was sleeping between two soldiers, bound by chains. Soldiers guarded the entrance. Suddenly an angel of the Lord appeared and a light shone in the prison cell. The angel struck Peter's side to wake him.

"Get up!" the angel said. Then the chains fell from Peter's wrists. "Put on your clothes and sandals," the angel said. "Follow me."

Peter did what the angel said and followed him from the prison. The iron gate opened and they walked down the street. Then the angel disappeared.

Peter headed for the house of Mary, John Mark's mother. Christians were praying there for Peter. Peter knocked on the courtyard door and a servant girl named Rhoda answered. She knew it was Peter's voice and was so happy that she ran to tell the others. Rhoda was so excited she forgot to open the door.

"Peter is at the door!" she cried out.

"You're crazy," the others said. "It must be his angel." But she insisted that he was there, and Peter kept on knocking. At last they let him in. Then Peter had them be quiet. After he told them what had happened, he left.

There was quite a stir the next day at the prison. Herod executed the guards, then went to Caesarea where he put on royal robes and gave a speech.

"This is a god!" some people shouted. Herod accepted their praise, but God was angry and struck him down with worms so that he died.

Paul Begins His Travels for Jesus

"I have a special work for Barnabas and Saul," the Holy Spirit said. The Christians at Antioch prayed and put their hands on these two men. Then they sent them on a trip. These men would tell people in other countries about Jesus. John Mark went with them.

They went to Seleucia, Cyprus, Salamis, and Paphos. The governor of Paphos, Sergius Paulus, invited the men to tell him about Jesus. But a magician named Elymas tried to keep the governor from believing.

"You are working against God," Paul told him. "God will make you blind for a while." Suddenly Elymas was blind, begging for someone to lead him.

The next stop was Perga. For some reason John Mark left Paul and Barnabas and went home to Jerusalem.

Paul and Barnabas went on to Antioch in Pisidia. On the Sabbath they went to the synagogue. Paul preached a sermon about Jesus. "He is the Messiah, God's Son," Paul said.

Paul and Barnabas went back the next Sabbath. Almost everyone in town went too. But the Jews were jealous when they saw the big crowd. They argued with Paul and insulted him.

"We had to bring the good news to you first," Paul told them. "But you have rejected it. Now we will take it to the Gentiles." The Gentiles were glad to hear this. Many of them believed. Then the Jews stirred up trouble and made Paul and Barnabas leave town.

Paul and Barnabas Are Mistaken for Gods

There was a crippled man in Lystra who had never walked. While Paul preached, the man listened. Paul watched and knew he could be healed.

"Stand on your feet!" Paul shouted.

The man jumped up and walked. This was an amazing miracle. The people of Lystra began to shout, "The gods have come to us. They look like men, but they are gods."

The people called Paul "Hermes" and they called Barnabas "Zeus." There was a temple of Zeus just outside town. The priest brought bulls and flowers. He and the people wanted to offer these to Paul and Barnabas as a sacrifice.

Paul and Barnabas tore their clothes when they saw this. "Why are you doing this?" they said. "We are only people, like you. We are here to tell you the good news about Jesus."

The people of Lystra still wanted to make a sacrifice to them.

Then some men came from Antioch. Others came from Iconium. They said bad things about Paul and Barnabas. The people of Lystra believed them. Then they threw stones at Paul and dragged him out of town. They thought he was dead.

But the Christians came to help Paul. He got up and went back into Lystra. The next day he and Barnabas went on to Derbe.

Paul Is Called to Macedonia

Paul and Barnabas had an argument. Barnabas wanted John Mark to come with them again. Paul did not want him. So Barnabas chose John Mark to go with him. Paul chose Silas to go with him.

Paul and Silas went through Derbe to Lystra. A believer named Timothy lived there. He had a Jewish mother and a Greek father. All the Christians in Lystra and Iconium said good things about Timothy.

Paul wanted to take Timothy with him. So he circumcised him. The Jews in the towns where they were going knew Timothy's father was Greek. They would not accept him unless he was circumcised.

Paul, Timothy, and Silas traveled from town to town. They met with the believers. They told the believers what the apostles and elders in Jerusalem had decided. They told them the rules for the new churches. These churches grew stronger and larger each day.

Paul and his friends went through Phrygia and Galatia. The Holy Spirit did not let them preach in the area called Asia.

One night at the town of Troas, Paul had a vision. In the vision a Macedonian man begged, "Come over to Macedonia and help us."

Paul was sure that this was God's way of telling them what to do. So he and his friends got ready to go.

Lydia Becomes a Christian

Paul and his friends went from Troas to Macedonia by ship. Their first stop was the island of Samothrace. Then they sailed for the seaport called Neapolis. From there they walked to Philippi.

Philippi was the most important city of that part of Macedonia. It was also a Roman colony.

Paul and his friends stayed several days at Philippi. On the Sabbath they went to the riverside outside town. They thought they would find some Jews gathered there for prayer.

There was a group of women by the river. One of them was Lydia, who sold purple cloth. She believed in God and worshiped Him.

Lydia listened carefully to Paul. She believed in Jesus and asked Paul to baptize her and the other people in her house.

"Stay with us in my house," Lydia told Paul and his friends. "If you think I'm truly a Christian, please stay."

Paul and his friends stayed with Lydia at her house. It was good to have a home and food in a strange place. Paul and his friends must have been thankful, don't you think?

The Prison at Philippi

Paul and his friends stayed several days at Philippi. One day as they were going to pray a slave girl met them. She had an evil spirit in her. The girl's owners made much money because this girl was a fortune-teller.

"In Jesus' name, I command you to come out of that girl!" Paul shouted. The evil spirit came out at that moment.

The girl's owners were angry. They knew they could not make money with the girl now. So they grabbed Paul and Silas and dragged them to the town officials in the public square. "These Jews are causing trouble here," they said. "They are teaching things against our law. We cannot let them do this." Soon the crowd that had gathered was against Paul and Silas.

The officials tore the clothes from Paul and Silas. They had them beaten and thrown into the inner prison with large blocks of wood fastened to their feet.

About midnight Paul and Silas were praying and singing. The other prisoners listened. Suddenly an earthquake shook the prison. The doors opened, and the chains fell from the prisoners. When the jailer saw this he tried to kill himself. He would be tortured if he let these men escape.

"Don't hurt yourself." Paul said. "We are all here."

Then the jailer rushed in with a light, he fell down before Paul and Silas. He was trembling. "What must I do to be saved?" he asked.

"Believe in the Lord Jesus," Paul answered. "Then you and your family will be saved." Paul then told the jailer and the others in his house about Jesus.

The jailer washed their wounds. Then he and his family were baptized. The jailer and his family were happy now because they were Christians.

The Bereans Accept Paul

Wherever Paul went, someone tried to hurt him. There were many people who did not want others to believe in Jesus.

When Paul visited Thessalonica, the same thing happened. Some people stirred up the crowd around them. They got Paul and his friends in a lot of trouble.

The Christians at Thessalonica sent Paul and his friends to Berea one night. Paul went to the synagogue to preach, as he always did in a town.

The people at Berea listened carefully to Paul. They were not against him like others had been. Each day they studied the Bible to see if the things Paul said were true.

Many of the people of Berea became Christians. Some of these new Christians were important Greek men and women.

But Paul's enemies in Thessalonica came to Berea. They stirred up trouble. So the Christians in Berea sent Paul to the coast. Silas and Timothy stayed in Berea a while.

Some Bereans went with Paul as far as Athens, in Greece. When they came back to Berea, they brought a message from Paul. "Come and join me as soon as possible," Paul told Silas and Timothy.

Paul at Mars Hill

Paul was waiting in Athens for Silas and Timothy. As he looked around the city he became upset at the many idols he saw.

At the synagogue, Paul talked to Jews and Greeks who worshiped God. He also went to the marketplace each day to talk with the people there.

Some Epicurean and Stoic teachers argued with Paul. But he told them the good news, how Jesus rose from the dead.

"He's dreaming," they said. "He doesn't know what he is saying. He must be teaching about some foreign religion."

These men took Paul to Mars Hill. It was also called Areopagus. The city council was there. These men wanted to hear what Paul was saying. "We want to know what these things mean," they said. People in Athens spent most of their time talking about new things.

Paul spoke to the city council. "You people of Athens are very religious," he said. "You even have an altar to an unknown god." Then Paul talked about God and His Son Jesus.

When the people of Athens heard Paul talk about Jesus' being raised from the dead, some made fun of him. Others asked to hear him again. One council member became a Christian, along with a woman named Damaris, and some others.

Diana of the Ephesians

A riot started in Ephesus because of the Christians. This is the way it happened. A silversmith named Demetrius made silver models of the goddess Diana's temple. Sometimes she was called Artemis.

Demetrius made much money from this business. So did other silversmiths who worked with him.

One day Demetrius called his fellow workers together. "You know that we make much money from this business," he told them. "But Paul is hurting our sales. He is also telling people that Diana and her temple are not important."

This made the men angry. "Diana is very important," they shouted. They stirred up a mob and grabbed Gaius and Aristarchus, two of Paul's friends from Macedonia. The mob rushed to the big open theater.

Paul wanted to go there and talk to the mob. But his friends would not let him. A man named Alexander tried to talk, but the mob would not listen to him because he was a Jew. The mob kept shouting, "Diana is great! Diana is great!" They kept doing that for two hours.

At last the city clerk stopped the shouting. "Everyone knows that Ephesus is the center where Diana is worshiped," he said. "So why make such a fuss about it? These men haven't done anything. If Demetrius and his friends have a problem, they should take it to the courts. The judges will do what is right. Or our town meeting can handle it. If the Roman government demands to know why we are rioting, I don't know what to tell them. Now please go home."

So the people went home. The silversmith riot was over.

Eutychus Falls from a Window

Paul was on his way home to Jerusalem. Timothy and some other friends had gone ahead. They had stopped a while at Troas. Then Paul and some other friends joined them five days later and spent a week.

On Saturday night Paul led a communion service. This was in a room on the third floor of a building. The room was lit with many oil lamps, and so the room became quite warm.

Paul preached a long sermon. He kept preaching until midnight. That was the last day he would spend with these people. He had many things to say to them.

A young man named Eutychus was sitting in the large open window. As Paul kept on preaching, Eutychus could hardly stay awake. He fell asleep and dropped to the ground, three stories below.

Everyone rushed downstairs, but Eutychus was dead. Paul went down, too. He took Eutychus in his arms.

"Don't worry," Paul told the Christians. "Eutychus is alive now."

Then everyone went back upstairs. They finished the communion service. But Paul preached again until early morning. Then he left.

Now the people went home. They were certainly happy that Eutychus was alive and well.

Paul Is Arrested

When Paul went back to Jerusalem, he visited the temple. But some people of Asia who hated him saw him there. They began to shout. "Help! This man is doing bad things here in our holy temple," they shouted.

A mob rushed at Paul and dragged him out of the temple. Then the temple doors were closed. The mob began to beat Paul. They wanted to kill him, but some Roman soldiers came and took him away.

The Roman commander put Paul in chains. "Who is he and what has he done?" he asked. But he got many answers. "Away with him," the mob kept shouting. The next day the commander took Paul to the council of religious leaders. He wanted to find why Paul was in trouble. When Paul said he was a Pharisee, the Pharisees were for him, and the Sadducees were against him.

The following day more than 40 men plotted together. They would not eat or drink until they had killed Paul. Paul's nephew, the son of Paul's sister, heard about this and told the army commander.

By nine that night the commander left Jerusalem with 200 soldiers and 70 horsemen and 200 spearmen. They took Paul with them on a horse.

Commander Claudius Lysias sent a letter with Paul and the soldiers. It told Governor Felix at Caesarea why Paul was sent to him.

That night the group camped at Antipatris. The foot soldiers came back to Jerusalem the next day and the others took Paul to Caesarea. They turned Paul over to Governor Felix and went home.

"I will hear you when your accusers come," the governor said. Then he put Paul with guards in the palace built by Herod.

Paul Before Governors and Kings

Paul was in prison in the palace at Caesarea. Five days after he went there Ananias came with other religious leaders. Ananias had been the high priest before his son-in-law Caiaphas.

These men brought an orator named Tertullus. He said that Paul was a troublemaker. He said that Paul was trying to hurt the temple.

Governor Felix let Paul speak next. Paul said he had done nothing wrong. If he did, what was it?

Felix kept Paul guarded after the trial. But he let him have more freedom. He even asked Paul to tell him about Jesus from time to time. After two long years, Porcius Festus became governor in place of Felix.

Festus had another trial. Again the religious leaders from Jerusalem came. Again they spoke lies about Paul. "Will you go to Jerusalem to be tried?" Festus asked.

"No, I want Caesar to judge me," Paul answered. He knew he would not get a fair trial in Jerusalem with those men.

Since Paul was a Roman citizen, he could ask Caesar to judge him. So Festus agreed to let him go to Rome to see Caesar.

A few days later King Agrippa and Bernice came to Caesarea. Agrippa wanted to hear Paul. So Paul was brought before him. When Agrippa heard Paul he said, "He has done nothing wrong. He could be set free if he had not asked to go to Caesar."

Plans were made to send Paul to Rome. There he would be tried by the Roman Emperor, who was called Caesar.

Paul Sails and Is Shipwrecked

Paul had asked Caesar, the Roman Emperor, to judge him. He knew he would not get a fair trial in Jerusalem. The religious leaders there hated him. So plans were made to send Paul to Rome.

Julius, an officer in the emperor's army, guarded Paul and some other prisoners. Julius was kind to Paul. When the ship came to Sidon, he let Paul visit friends. They gave Paul what he needed for his trip.

But sailing was hard. The wind was blowing toward the ship. It took much longer than they thought. By the time the ship reached Fair Havens, on the island of Crete, it was getting too late to sail. The sea would soon be dangerous.

One day a strong "Northeaster" wind blew. It blew them far off course. For 14 days the storm kept up. All 276 men on the ship thought they would die.

One night the ship came near land. The sailors put out the anchors. They threw all the grain from the ship into the sea. Then they waited for morning.

When morning came the sailors saw land. They cut the ropes to the anchors. They sailed for the land. But the ship hit a sandbar and broke into pieces. Some men swam to shore. Others floated on boards.

It was raining and cold when the men came to land, an island called Malta. The people built a fire to warm the men.

Suddenly a poisonous snake came from some sticks and bit Paul. When he did not die the people thought he was a god. The shipwrecked people stayed three months on this island. An important man named Publius took care of them. Paul healed Publius's father. He also healed others on the island. So the people were kind to Paul and the other men. They gave them all they needed.

Paul at Rome

A ship from Alexandria had stayed at Malta for the winter. When it was time to go, this ship took Paul and the others toward Rome. They landed at a port called Puteoli. From there Paul would be taken to Rome on one of the Roman roads.

Some Christians came to meet Paul. They asked Paul to stay with them for a week. Then they went on toward Rome. When they were about 40 miles from Rome, some Christians from Rome came to meet them. This was a place called the Appii Forum. Others joined them at a place called the Three Inns. Paul thanked God for these Christians. He felt much better when he saw them.

In Rome, Paul was allowed to live by himself, but he had a Roman guard with him at all times. Many people came to see him. He told them about Jesus.

Three days after Paul arrived, he invited the Jewish leaders in Rome to meet with him. He told them about Jesus and showed them how the Old Testament was about Him. Some of them became Christians. Others would not believe.

For two years, Paul lived in Rome, waiting for his trial. While he was there, he told many people the good news about Jesus. He had great courage and did not worry about getting into trouble. And no one kept him from teaching and preaching about Jesus.

Collect All 8
Children's All-time Favorite Bible Stories

Noah and the Great Flood

Moses Is Born

David and Goliath

Daniel in the Lion's Den

Jesus Is Born

The Good Samaritan

Jesus Is Raised from the Dead

Paul Sails and Is Shipwrecked

www.ingramcontent.com/pod-product-compliance
Lightning Source LLC
Chambersburg PA
CBHW061800290426
44109CB00030B/2905